MUFFIN REC
YOU MUST BAKE!
(at least once in your life)

Essential and Awesome Recipes

by Mary Black

Table of Contents

Introduction

Once upon a time...

Somewhere between bread and cupcakes, lies the enchanted land of muffins. Either savory or sweet, muffins lend themselves to endless variations and can (and should) be eaten any time of day.

Once you learn the basic muffin method (incorporating dry ingredients into wet), you can begin to experiment with all kinds of flavor combinations.

Throw in a handful of berries, fruit, nuts, a few dashes of spices and plain muffins are transformed into something magical. Add a crumb, strudel or frosting-like topping for some texture. Drizzle with caramel or smear with a nut butter for some variety. Take the whole thing a savory route by incorporating corn, jalapenos, carrots, zucchini or cheese.

Even the strongest willed can't resist a warm, straight-from-the-oven muffin, no matter the flavor.

Bake up a batch today and share some muffin love with your friends (or just yourself, nobody's watching).

Better Blueberry Muffins

Packed with succulent berries, these muffins burst with juicy blueberry flavor with every bite. The crumbly, sweet topping has just the right hint of spicy nutmeg to create a balanced flavor profile. If using frozen blueberries, do not thaw them before baking as the juices will run throughout the muffin affecting its texture and presentation.

Ingredients:

1 1/3 cups (160 g) all-purpose flour

1 large egg

1/3 cup (80 g) butter or margarine, at room temp

2/3 cup (130 g) granulated sugar

2/3 teaspoon (3 ml) vanilla

1 1/3 teaspoons (6 g) baking powder

1/4 teaspoon (2 g) salt

1/3 cup (80 ml) milk

1 2/3 cups (250 g) fresh or frozen blueberries

Topping:

2/3 tablespoon (10 g) granulated sugar, mixed with

1/4 teaspoon (1 g) ground nutmeg

Directions:

Preheat the hot box to 375° (190° C) while you gather your ingredients.

Lightly grease a muffin pan to accommodate 12 muffins.

In a large bowl, cream butter then add sugar and whip until it up until the mixture reaches a light and airy consistency.

Carefully incorporate eggs, one at a time. Make sure to fully beat in each egg before adding the next one. This will dramatically change the consistency of your muffins.

Once you have added all of the eggs, beat in vanilla, baking powder and salt.

Using a wooden spoon or rubber spatula, gently fold in half of flour until no lumps remain. Then, fold in half of milk. Repeat this step with the other half of the flour and milk.

Gently fold in blueberries. Do not over-mix. You want the batter to remain fluffy so that the final muffins bake up light and moist.

Carefully spoon the batter into your muffin tin, distributing the batter evenly amongst 12 cups and sprinkle each muffin with the topping.

Bake 15 to 20 minutes or until golden on top. The muffins should rise a bit and will bounce back when lightly touched.

Big Bad (as in really good) Blueberry Muffins

The big mama of blueberry muffins, these baked pleasure bites are large and overflowing with blueberry goodness. Fill your muffins cups all the way up to get that crusty, overflowing muffin top that baked dreams are made of.

Ingredients:

2-1/4 cups (270 g) all-purpose flour

2 eggs

1 cup and 2 tablespoons (225 g) white sugar

3/4 teaspoon (5 g) salt

1 tablespoon (15 g) baking powder

1/2 cup (120 ml) vegetable oil

1/2 cup (120 ml) milk

1-1/2 cups (225 g) fresh blueberries

1/2 cup (60 g) all-purpose flour

Topping:

1/3 cup (40 g) flour

¼ cup (60 g) butter

½ cup (100 g) sugar

1 ½ teaspoons (8 g) cinnamon

Directions:

Heat your oven to 400 ° F (200 ° C). Grease muffin tins with butter or line them with liners.

In a large bowl, combine flour, sugar, salt and baking powder. Stir together until everything is evenly mixed.

In a separate bowl, combine vegetable oil, eggs and cup of milk.

Incorporate the wet ingredients into the dry. Do not over-mix. Just stir enough to combine.

Gently fold in the blueberries.

Pour batter into muffin tins, filling each right up to the top.

Make topping mixture by combining all of the topping ingredients in a small bowl and mixing with your fingers lightly until it takes on a crumb-like consistency.

Sprinkle topping generously on top of each muffin.

Bake for 20 to 25 minutes or until golden brown and fluffy.

Volcanic Chocolate Muffins

This recipe takes a little work but the pay off is explosive. Perhaps, prepare these for a dinner party or just impress yourself with your newfangled abilities to create gooey, volcanic magic.

Ingredients:

3 tablespoons (45 g) flour

4 eggs

1 stick (113 g) butter

1/2 cup (100 g) sugar

8 ounces (230 g) semisweet chocolate chips

1/2 teaspoon (3 ml) vanilla extract

1/4 teaspoon (2 g) salt

Butter, to coat muffin tin

1 tablespoon (15 g) cocoa powder

1 cup (240 g) vanilla ice cream

1 teaspoon (5 g) espresso powder

Directions:

Heat your oven to 375 ° F (190 ° C).

Place the chocolate and butter in a small metal bowl. Create a double broiler by placing the bowl over a pan with a bit of simmering water. The steam that rises will melt the chocolate and butter gently. Alternatively, you can melt them in the microwave at 10 second intervals to prevent burning.

Once your combine the melted butter and chocolate, stir in vanilla and set aside.

Combine sugar, flour and salt in a large bowl. Sift these ingredients into the melted chocolate mixture and combine fully using an electric hand mixer.

Drop in eggs one at time, making sure to fully incorporate each egg before adding in the next one.

Once all of the eggs are added, continue to beat the batter on high for about 4 minutes or until it is creamy and turns a pale color.

Chill the batter in the refrigerator while you prepare the muffin tins.

Lightly grease each muffin cup with butter and dust with a thin layer of the cocoa powder (shake out any excess powder).

Remove batter from the fridge once it has had a little time to rest (20-30 minutes) and drop it into the pan with a small scoop.

Bake for 10 to 11 minutes.

These muffins should have a gooey center and have a cake-like exterior. As such, the typical toothpick test will not work here. Just follow the directions closely and do not leave in the oven longer than indicated or else they will burn.

While muffins are baking, use a small saucepan to melt the ice cream. Once melted, stir in the espresso powder.

Drizzle over muffins.

Chocolate Chip Muffins

or sweet with these warm, chocolate bombs. The nuts create little crunch well in combination with the chocolate chips. You might as well go all the way and decorize them with a swipe of Nutella or serve warm with a scoop of vanilla ice cream.

Ingredients:

2 cups (240 g) all-purpose flour

2 eggs , lightly beaten

1/2 cup butter (120 g) , melted and cooled

1/3 cup light-brown sugar (60 g), packed

1/3 cup (65 g) sugar

2 teaspoons (10 g) baking powder

1/2 teaspoon (4 g) salt

2/3 cup (160 ml) milk

1 teaspoon (5 ml) vanilla

1 (11 1/2 ounce/326 g) package milk chocolate chips

1/2 cup (75 g) walnuts or pecans , chopped

Directions:

Heat your oven to 400°F (204 °C) while you make the batter.

Grease a 12 muffin tin.

Sift together flour, sugars, baking powder, and salt in a large bowl.

In a smaller bowl, mix your wet ingredients by stirring together milk, eggs, butter, and vanilla until well combined.

Create a little well in center of dry ingredients and add in your wet ingredients until they are just combined. Careful not to over-mix.

Gently fold in chocolate chips and nuts with a wooden spoon or rubber spatula.

Fill greased muffin tins with batter.

Bake for 15-20 minutes or until. Insert a toothpick into the center of one muffin and if it comes out clean, your muffins are done.

Cool muffin tin on a wire rack for 5 minutes. Then remove muffins from tin to cool completely.

Nutty 'Nana Muffins

These muffins are sweet without a ton of sugar because of the bananas in the recipe. Don't be afraid to use really brown bananas. Very ripe bananas lend this recipe the best flavor as they sugar content becomes more concentrated and they impart more banana flavor the riper they are. The little brown banana ribbons that run through the muffin make it irresistible.

Ingredients

2 cups (240 g) all-purpose flour

2 eggs

3/4 cup (180 g) (1 1/2 sticks) unsalted butter, melted and cooled

1 cup (180 g) brown sugar

1 1/2 teaspoons (8 g) baking soda

1/2 teaspoon (4 g) salt

4 overripe bananas

1 teaspoon (5 ml) pure vanilla extract

1/2 cup (75 g) pecans, chopped

Directions:

Heat the oven to 375 °F (190 °C) and lightly grease a 12 muffin tin.

Sift flour, baking soda, and salt into a large bowl.

In another bowl, use a fork to mash two of the bananas. Don't pulverize them; just mash lightly leaving a little texture.

In the bowl of an electric mixer fitted with a wire whisk attachment, whip the rest of the bananas and sugar vigorously for 3 minutes until frothy.

Add in the melted butter, eggs, and vanilla and beat well. Using a rubber spatula, scrape down the sides a couple of times to get everything incorporated evenly.

Slowly add the dry ingredients until just blended making sure you don't over-mix as this will compromise the fluffy consistency of the finished muffins.

Turn off the mixer and gently fold in the mashed bananas and nuts with a rubber spatula.

Fill the muffin tins about halfway with the batter and tap them lightly on the counter to knock out air bubbles.

Bake for 18 to 20 minutes or until a toothpick inserted into the center of one muffin comes out clean.

Let cool in muffin tin on a wire rack for 5 minutes.

Turn the tin out and continue cooling the muffins for a few more minutes (if you can resist eating them at this point that is).

Serve warm with a little peanut butter on the side.

Crumbly Banana Bliss Muffins

Sweet banana bread-like muffins, the crumbly topping is what really seals the deal. A combination of crunchy sugar and cinnamon bits, the topping melts in your mouth as the banana flavors roll around on your tongue. Stop drooling; start baking.

Ingredients:

1 1/2 cups (180 g) all-purpose flour

1 egg, lightly beaten

1/3 cup (80 ml) butter, melted

3/4 cup (150 g) white sugar

1/3 cup (60 g) packed brown sugar

1 teaspoon (5 g) baking soda

1 teaspoon (5 g) baking powder

1/2 teaspoon (4 g) salt

3 bananas, mashed

2 tablespoons (15 g) all-purpose flour

1/8 teaspoon (0.6 g) ground cinnamon

1 tablespoon (15 g) butter

Directions:

Set oven to 375 ° F (190 ° C) and preheat while you prepare the batter.

Lightly grease 12 muffin cups or line a tin with 12 muffin liners.

Sift 1 1/2 cups flour, baking soda, baking powder and salt in a large bowl and set aside (dry ingredients).

In a different bowl, cream bananas, sugar, egg and melted butter (wet ingredients).

Incorporate your wet ingredients into the dry ingredients and stir just until combined (not more!).

Distribute batter evenly amongst the 12 prepared muffin cups.

To prepare the crumb topping, combine brown sugar, 2 tablespoons (about 29 g) flour and cinnamon in a small bowl. Use your finders to massage in1 tablespoon butter until the mixture looks like large crumb granules.

Sprinkle crumbs over the top of every muffin generously.

Bake for 18 to 20 minutes or until a tester comes out clean when inserted into center of a muffin.

Fresh Pumpkin Muffins

While many pumpkin muffins are made with the canned stuff, these take a little elbow grease to make as they use fresh sugar pumpkins. Some people swear that there is no difference between the canned and fresh variety. Try these for yourself before forming an opinion. Hint: They're better fresh. Always.

Ingredients:

3 cups (360 g) all-purpose flour

3 eggs

2 cups (400 g) white sugar

1 small sugar pumpkin, seeded

2 teaspoons (10 g) baking soda

1/2 teaspoon (3 g) baking powder

2 teaspoons (10 g) ground cloves

2 teaspoons (10 g) ground cinnamon

2 teaspoons (10 g) ground nutmeg

1 teaspoon (5 g) ground allspice

1 teaspoon (8 g) salt

2/3 cup (160 ml) vegetable oil

Directions:

Preheat oven to 350 ° F (175 ° C). Grease 12 muffin cups or line with paper muffin liners.

Butcher your pumpkin like a pro. Start by popping the pumpkin in half and putting each piece, cut side down, on a baking sheet. Use a large piece of foil to cover the entire pan and bake the pumpkin until you can easily pierce the flesh with a knife (about 1 1/3 hours). Take the pumpkin out (leave the oven on) and let rest until cool to the touch. Use a large spoon to scoop out its guts and puree the flesh in a blender until smooth. You will only be using 2 cups (about 450 g) of the puree so make some plans for the rest (pumpkin smoothie?)

Combine flour, sugar, baking soda, baking powder, cloves, cinnamon, nutmeg, allspice and salt in a large bowl.

In another bowl, mix 2 cups (about 450 g) pumpkin puree, vegetable oil and eggs with a wire whisk.

Stir wet ingredients into dry ingredients just until moistened.

Pour mixture into greased muffin tins.

Bake for 20 to 25 minutes. To check if your muffins are ready, insert a toothpick into the center of one and see if it comes out clean.

Remove from oven and cool on wire rack for 5 minutes before turning out.

Serve warm. To go overboard on pumpkin, slather the top with homemade pumpkin butter. Use the remaining pumpkin puree to make pumpkin butter by melting equal parts brown sugar, a dash of each of the spices you used for the muffin recipe and pumpkin puree in a small saucepan on low heat until it forms a paste. Let the mixture cool and store in an airtight container in the refrigerator.

Amazing Apple Pie Muffins

Everyone knows the classic flavors of apple pie: cinnamon, butter, brown sugar and juicy, tart apples. Well, these muffins pack them into a carry-anywhere pie so you can throw them into a picnic basket, your kids' lunch bag for dessert or any other welcoming receptacle (like your mouth).

Ingredients:

2 1/2 cups (300 g) all-purpose flour

1 egg

1 1/2 cups (270 g) firmly packed brown sugar

2/3 cup (160 ml) vegetable oil

1 1/2 teaspoons (8 ml) vanilla

1 teaspoon (5 g) cinnamon

1 teaspoon (5 g) baking soda

1/4 teaspoon (2 g) salt

1 cup (240 ml) buttermilk

2 cups (300 g) diced peeled firm tart apples (such as Spy, Granny Smith or Pink Lady)

Topping:

1/3 cup (40 g) all-purpose flour

1/4 cup (60 g) unsalted butter, melted

1/2 cup (90 g) firmly packed brown sugar

1 teaspoon (5 g) cinnamon

Directions:

Preheat the oven to 350°F (180 ° C).

Make the topping by mixing sugar, flour, butter and cinnamon in a small bowl with your fingers until a coarse crumble forms. Set aside.

With a wire whisk, combine brown sugar, oil, egg and vanilla in a large bowl. Mix until smooth.

Sift flour, baking soda and salt in a smaller bowl.

Incorporate your wet ingredients into the dry and stir in buttermilk until a thin, uniform batter forms.

Gently fold in apple pieces just until combined. Careful not to over-mix.

Pour batter into greased muffin tin (the larger cup variety) filling each cup about 3/4 of the way up.

Sprinkle each muffin generously and evenly with topping.

Bake 25-30 minutes or until golden brown and top bounces back when touched lightly.

Apple Strudel Muffins

The only thing that can make apple strudel better is throwing a heaping, crumble of sugar and cinnamon on top and turning the whole thing into a moist muffin. These are simple to make, fun to eat and good to share. Bake a batch and watch your social network expand by 12 servings.

Ingredients:

2 cups (240 g) all-purpose flour

2 eggs

1/2 cup (120 g) butter

1 cup (200 g) white sugar

1 teaspoon (5 g) baking powder

1/2 teaspoon (3 g) baking soda

1/2 teaspoon (4 g) salt

1 1/4 teaspoons (6 ml) vanilla

1 1/2 cups (200 g) chopped apples

Topping:

1 tablespoon (8g) all-purpose flour

1 tablespoon (15 g) butter

1/3 cup (60 g) packed brown sugar

1/8 teaspoon (0.6 g) ground cinnamon

Directions:

Heat oven to 375 ° F (190 ° C) and lightly grease a 12 cup muffin pan with butter.

Sift flour, baking powder, baking soda and salt in a medium bowl.

Cream butter, sugar and eggs in a larger bowl until smooth. Stir in vanilla.

Stir in apples.

Add your dry ingredients gradually until well incorporated.

Pour batter into the prepared muffin pan, filling each muffin cup about ¾ of the way up.

Stir together brown sugar, flour and cinnamon in a small bowl. Cut in butter until the mixture takes on a coarse crumbly consistency.

Sprinkle crumbs generously over tops of muffin batter.

Bake 20 minutes or until the tops are toasty brown. Allow to rest for 5 minutes before taking muffins out of the pan.

This step will be hard: Cool on a wire rack completely before serving.

Suggestion: add ¼ cup (about 2 g) of walnuts or pecans into batter before baking to give these a nice crunch.

Berry Bran Muffins

The ultimate breakfast muffin, the bran cereal gives these muffins some nutritional punch by adding a dose of filling fiber. Add a variety of berries for a morning meal that will get you through to lunch without hunger pangs. While buttermilk in this recipe lends a lot of moisture to the batter, even the moistest bran muffins can be chewier than regular muffins. To compliment the denser texture, serve with a glass of milk or your choice of fruit spread.

Ingredients:

1/2 cup (60 g) all-purpose white flour

1/2 cup (60 g) whole wheat flour

1 large egg , beaten

3/4 cup (135 g) brown sugar , packed

1 1/2 cups (90 g) all-bran cereal

1 cup (240 ml) buttermilk (low-fat or full)

1/3 cup (80 ml) vegetable oil (or melted butter)

2 teaspoons (10 ml) maple extract or vanilla extract

1 1/4 teaspoons (6g) baking powder

1 teaspoon (5 g) baking soda

1/2 teaspoon (4 g) salt

1/2 teaspoon (3 g) cinnamon

1/4 teaspoon (1 g) ground nutmeg

1 cup (150 g) raisins (or chopped dates, blueberries, blackberries, golden raisins or a 1 cup combination of all)

Directions:

Heat oven to 350°F (180°C).

Lightly grease 12 muffin cups.

Soak the All-Bran cereal in buttermilk in a medium sized bowl for about 10-12 minutes, stirring once halfway through.

In a separate bowl, mix oil, egg, brown sugar and vanilla until incorporated. Using a wooden spoon, add in the buttermilk mixture.

In a large, clean bowl, stir together flour, baking powder, baking soda, salt, cinnamon and nutmeg.

Slowly pour wet mixture into the dry ingredients. Using either a rubber spatula or wooden spoon, stir to combine into a batter just until moistened. A couple of small lumps are fine; do not over-mix or the muffins will be dense and dry.

Gently fold in your choice of raisins or berries (or both).

Spoon batter into 12 muffin cups. Fill evenly.

Bake for 18-22 minutes and to make sure your muffins are done, insert a toothpick in the center and if it comes out clean, you can remove them from the oven.

Old Fashioned Bran Muffins

If a bowl of cereal is just not cutting it anymore, liven it up by using it to make a delicious muffin instead. This simple recipe reinvents boring bran cereal and creates a portable breakfast or snack that fills you with healthy fiber. Bran muffins tend to be a litter drier and denser than other muffins so moisten things up by splitting the muffin open while warm and slathering it with butter or jam. For something a little extra special, add a pinch of cinnamon to your buttered muffin and broil in the oven for 2-3 minutes, cut side up, until toasty and crispy on the edges and chewy in the middle.

Ingredients:

1 1/3 cups (160 g) all-purpose flour

1 egg

1/2 cup (100 g) sugar

1 tablespoon (15g) baking powder

1 teaspoon (8 g) salt

1 1/2 cups (90 g) Kellogg's All-Bran Original cereal or All-Bran Buds

1 cup (240 ml) milk

1/3 cup (65 g) shortening or vegetable oil (80 ml)

Directions:

Preheat oven to 400 ° F (200 ° C). Lightly coat 12 muffin cups with cooking spray.

Mix flour, sugar, baking powder and salt in a medium bowl.

Soak cereal in milk in a larger bowl for about 2 minutes or until cereal absorbs some of the milk and softens.

Beat in egg and shortening.

Gently stir in flour mixture until just combined.

Portion batter evenly into prepared muffin cups.

Bake for approximately 25 minutes. The muffins should be golden brown and springy to the touch when done.

These can also be made stickier with molasses. Just reduce milk to ½ cup (120 ml) and replace with ½ cup (120 ml) of molasses when soaking the cereal. Completely omit the sugar called for in the recipe and follow the rest of the directions unchanged.

Sneaky Zucchini Muffins

These are a great way to get non-vegetable eaters to scarf down some green. The zucchini adds a delicate flavor that tastes nothing like vegetables and a lot like delicious-ness. These muffins can be tweaked to create interesting flavor variations due to the mildness of the zucchini. Traditionally, zucchini pairs well with walnuts and pecans. But think outside of the muffin tin and fold in raspberries and chocolate chips or apricots and cranberries.

Ingredients:

2 1/4 cups (270 g) all-purpose flour

2 eggs, lightly beaten

1 cup (200 g) white sugar

1/4 cup (45 g) brown sugar

2 1/2 teaspoons (13 g) baking powder

1/2 teaspoon (3 g) baking soda

1 teaspoon (5 g) ground cinnamon

1 teaspoon (5 g) ground nutmeg

1/2 teaspoon (4 g) salt

1/2 cup (95 g) shortening

1/4 cup (60 ml) sour milk

1 1/2 cups (200 g) shredded zucchini

1 teaspoon (5 ml) vanilla extract

1/2 cup (75 g) chopped walnuts

Directions:

Heat oven to 350 ° F (175 ° C). Grease and lightly flour 12 muffin cups or use muffin liners.

Stir flour and sugar in a large bowl. Add in baking powder, baking soda, cinnamon, nutmeg and salt.

Using your fingers, cut in shortening until everything gets a little crumbly. Dig a well in the middle and add in milk, eggs, zucchini and vanilla.

Gently fold in walnuts.

Evenly distribute batter amongst the muffin cups, filling each about 2/3 to 3/4 of the way to the top.

Sprinkle a bit of brown sugar over the top of each muffin.

Bake for 15 to 20 minutes. To determine if your muffins are done, insert a toothpick into the center and if it comes out clean, they are ready to remove from the oven.

Allow to cool. Serve slightly warm all on their own.

Tropical Zucchini Muffins

Just because zucchini isn't very tropical, doesn't mean a zucchini muffin can't smell like vacation. The whole wheat flour makes these healthier than your average Joe muffin and the mango chunks and unsweetened coconut gives these a taste of the tropics. You can also fold in some pistachios for a bit of crunch and a little more green. Serve these with a pina colada and let yourself be transported to paradise.

Ingredients:

1 cup (120 g) whole-wheat flour

2/3 cup (80 g) all-purpose flour

1 large egg

1/2 cup (100 g) sugar

1 teaspoon (5 g) ground cinnamon

1 1/4 teaspoons (6 g) baking powder

1/2 teaspoon (3 g) baking soda

1/4 teaspoon (2 g) salt

1 1/3 cups (200 g) shredded zucchini

1/2 cup (120 ml) fat-free milk

2 tablespoons (30 ml) canola oil

2 tablespoons (30 ml) honey

½ cup (75 g) fresh mango, cubed

Cooking spray

Topping:

1 tablespoon (15 g) sugar

1/4 teaspoon (1g) ground cinnamon

¼ cup (15 g) unsweetened shredded coconut

Directions:

Heat oven to 400 °F (200 °C). Lightly spray 12 muffin cups with cooking spray.

Spoon flours into dry measuring cups lightly and level excess with a butter knife.

With a whisk, stir flours, sugar, baking soda, baking powder and salt in a large bowl.

In a small bowl, mix zucchini, milk, oil, honey, and egg until blended.

Make a well in center of the dry ingredients and add the wet ingredients just until combined.

Fold in mango cubes.

Spoon mixture into 12 prepared muffin cups.

Combine sugar, cinnamon and shredded coconut; sprinkle the mixture over tops of muffins.

Bake the muffins for 15 minutes or until golden brown.

Remove from oven and turn out onto a wire rack to cool.

Serve with a smile.

Moist and Sweet Carrot Muffins

A sweet way to add some beta carotene to your diet, these muffins are a moist and flavorful way to start the day. These can also easily be made vegan by replacing the egg with your choice of vegan egg replacer equivalent to one egg (flax, chia, mashed banana, etc.) and following the rest of the directions unchanged.

Ingredients:

1 cup (120 g) white flour

1 cup (120 g) whole wheat flour

1 egg

1/2 cup (100 g) sugar

3/4 cup (180 ml) orange juice

1/2 cup (120 ml) melted margarine

1 teaspoon (5 g) baking powder

1/2 teaspoon (3 g) baking soda

1/2 teaspoon (4 g) salt

1 teaspoon (5 g) cinnamon (more or less to taste)

2 cups (300 g) shredded carrots

Directions:

Preheat oven to 400 ° F (200 ° C).

Lightly whisk egg in a large bowl then beat in orange juice, margarine and sugar.

Sift together flours, baking powder, baking soda, salt and cinnamon.

Add dry ingredients into wet ingredients and incorporate only till moistened. Do not over-mix.

Lightly fold in shredded carrots (either finely grate them on a box grater or throw them in the food processor).

Divide amongst 12 muffin cups, filling each cup about 2/3 of the way.

Bake for 15-20 minutes or until muffins puff up and a toothpick inserted into the center comes out clean.

Stuff Your Face with Strawberry Muffins

Like a strawberry shortcake, only more nutritionally sound, you will have a hard time resisting the urge to stuff these whole into your mouth before letting them cool. The juicy, red strawberries baked up inside take on a compote consistency making every bite moist, flavorful and nothing short of joyful. An indulgent puff of whipped cream on top might be in order.

Ingredients:

1 1/4 cups (150 g) all-purpose flour

1 egg , beaten

1/2 cup (120 ml) butter (melted)

1/2 cup (100 g) sugar

2 1/2 teaspoons (13 g) baking powder

1/2 teaspoon (4 g) salt

1 cup (90 g) rolled oats

1 cup (240 ml) milk

1 teaspoon (5 ml) vanilla extract

1 cup strawberries (150 g), chopped

Directions:

Heat oven to 425 °F (220 °C) and lightly grease a 12 muffin tin.

In a large bowl, stir together flour, baking powder and salt.

Incorporate rolled oats and sugar. Set aside your dry ingredients.

In a smaller bowl, mix together milk, butter, egg and vanilla.

Combine wet ingredients and dry ingredients by adding milk mixture into flour mixture just until moistened.

Gently fold in strawberries.

Scoop batter into each muffin cup, filling each about 2/3 of the way up.

Bake 15 to 18 minutes. You can check if they're done by inserting a toothpick into the center and seeing if it comes out clean. The muffins should also be lightly brown in color when they're done.

Tangy Oatmeal Muffins

These muffins get their slight tang (and fluffiness) from buttermilk. Oatmeal is notoriously good with raisins and dried fruit. Since these muffins are like a delicious blank oatmeal slate, feel free to fold in nuts and dried fruit into the batter before putting them into the hot box.

Ingredients

1-1/2 cups (180 g) all-purpose flour

2 eggs, beaten

3/4 cup (135 g) packed brown sugar

1-1/2 cups (135 g) quick-cooking oats

1-1/2 cups (360 ml) buttermilk

1/4 cup and 2 tablespoons (90 ml) vegetable oil

1-1/2 teaspoons (8 g) baking powder

3/4 teaspoon (4 g) baking soda

3/4 teaspoon (5g) salt

Directions:

Preheat the oven to 400 ° F (200 °C). Either line 12 muffin cups with paper liners or grease 12 muffin cups with butter or cooking spray.

Start your batter by soaking oats in buttermilk in a medium-sized bowl for 15 minutes.

Once the oats are moist, add in egg, sugar and oil.

In a separate bowl, stir together flour, baking powder, baking soda and salt.

Incorporate flour mixture into oat mixture just until moistened. Do not over-mix.

Divide batter amongst 12 prepared muffin cups, filling about ¾ of the way up.

Bake for16-18 minutes or until a toothpick inserted into the center comes out clean.

Allow to rest in the muffin tin for about 5 minutes then turn out onto wire rack to finish cooling.

Aromatic Apple Muffins

Cinnamon and apple are classic autumn aroma (or winter, spring, anytime). When the leaves begin to turn and thoughts of curling up next to your warm oven begin to surface, nothing is more comforting than the aroma of spicy cinnamon and tart, juicy apples. Take a deep breath; this is going to smell amazing and taste even better.

Ingredients:

1 1/2 cups (180 g) flour

1 egg, slightly beaten

1/3 cup (80 ml) butter, melted

1/2 cup (100 g) sugar

1/2 cup (90 g) packed brown sugar

1 1/2 teaspoons (8 g) baking powder

1 teaspoon (5 g) ground cinnamon

1/2 cup (120 ml) milk

1 cup (150 g) finely chopped tart apples

Directions:

Heat oven to 375 °F (190 °C) and grease a 12 muffin tin.

Stir together flour, sugar, brown sugar, baking powder and cinnamon in a large bowl.

In the same bowl, add milk, butter, eggs and apples and give it a gentle stir until a loose batter forms.

Scoop batter into prepared muffin tin.

Bake at for19-23 minutes. The muffins should be light brown in color.

Cool inside the pan for about 5 minutes and loosen each muffin from the tin by running a dull blade around the edge (butter knife works well) before turning them out onto a wire rack to finish cooling.

Bursting with Berries Muffins

The orange zest here provides a nice contrast that brings out the flavor of whatever berries you choose to add in, making the flavors crisp and tart. If using frozen berries, make sure they aren't defrosted as the juices will bleed into the muffin batter creating a soupy mess.

Ingredients:

2 cups (240 g) flour

2 large eggs

1/2 cup (120 g) butter

3/4 cup (150 g) sugar

1 cup (240 ml) milk

1 1/2 teaspoons (8 g) orange zest

1 1/2 teaspoons (8 ml) vanilla extract

2 1/2 teaspoons (13 g) baking powder

3/4 teaspoon (5 g) salt

1 1/2 cups (225 g) fresh blueberries or frozen blueberries , unthawed (or raspberries, blackberries, a combination of all)

Directions:

Heat oven to 400 °F (200 °C) and line a 12 muffin pan with paper liners. You will want to use paper liners (as opposed to greasing the pan) as these muffins are moist due to the berries.

In a saucepan over medium heat, stir together milk, butter orange zest and vanilla extract until the butter melts. Cool the mixture until it is just slightly warm and then proceed to beat in the eggs. Make sure the mixture isn't too warm as you do not want to cook the eggs.

In a large bowl, stir together sifted flour, sugar, baking powder and salt.

Slowly incorporate wet ingredients from the saucepan into your dry ingredients just until combined. Do not over-mix.

Gently fold in whichever berries you are using.

Evenly divide the batter amongst the prepared muffin cups.

Bake for about 15-20 minutes or until a toothpick inserted into the center comes out clean and the muffins take on a golden brown color.

Sweet and Tart Cranberry Muffins

These muffins play a little flavor game in your mouth with every bite. The topping is sweet and spicy while the juicy cranberries are a toothsome burst of tartness. The sour cream plays off the flavor of the cranberries while giving these muffins a lot of moisture.

Ingredients:

2 cups (240 g) all-purpose flour

2 eggs

1/2 cup (120 g) butter or margarine, softened

1 cup (200 g) sugar

1 teaspoon (5 ml) vanilla extract

1 cup (240 g) sour cream

1 teaspoon (5 g) baking powder

1/2 teaspoon (3 g) baking soda

1/2 teaspoon (3 g) ground nutmeg

1/4 teaspoon (2 g) salt

1 cup (150 g) fresh or frozen cranberries

Topping:

2 tablespoons (25 g) sugar

1/8 teaspoon (0.6 g) ground nutmeg

Directions:

Preheat oven to 400 ° F (200 ° C)and grease or paper-line a 12 muffin tin.

Cream together butter and sugar in a large mixing bowl.

Incorporate eggs and vanilla until well-blended.

Gently fold the sour cream into the mixture.

In a separate bowl, stir together flour, baking powder, baking soda, nutmeg and salt,

Add dry ingredients into wet mixture just until a light batter forms.

Carefully fold in cranberries.

Pour batter into prepared muffin tins until about 2/3 of the way full.

Mix together sugar and nutmeg to create the topping and generously sprinkle over the top of the muffins.

Bake for 20-25 minutes or until a toothpick inserted into the center of one muffin comes out clean.

Allow to cool slightly (about 10 minutes) inside the pan before turning out onto a wire rack to finish cooling.

Pucker-Up Lemon Muffins

These muffins are all about contrasting sweet and sour. The glaze and sugary topping give them a necessary sweetness, like a lemon drop, that balances out the innate sour flavor of the lemon juice in the recipe. If you're more on the sweet side of things, consider using Meyer lemons, a variety that is much sweeter than its regular lemon counterpart.

Ingredients:

3 cups (360 g) all-purpose flour

4 eggs

1 cup (240 ml) butter, melted

2 cups (400 g) sugar

1/2 teaspoon (3 g) baking soda

1/2 teaspoon (4 g) salt

1 cup (240 g) sour cream

1 ½ tablespoons (21 g) grated lemon peel

1 tablespoon (15 ml) lemon juice

Topping:

1/3 cup (40 g) all-purpose flour

1/3 cup (65 g) sugar

1/8 cup (30 g) cold butter, cubed

Glaze:

1/4 cup (50 g) sugar

1/4 cup (60 ml) lemon juice

Directions:

Preheat oven to 350 ° F (180 ° C) and grease several muffin tins with either butter, cooking spray or line with paper muffin liners. This recipe yields 12 jumbo muffins.

Sift together flour, sugar, baking soda and salt in a large bowl.

Using a separate bowl, mix together eggs, sour cream, butter, lemon peel and juice.

Incorporate wet mixture into dry ingredients just until a light batter forms.

Pour batter into prepared muffin cups until they are about ¾ of the way full.

In a small, clean bowl, stir together flour and sugar. Using your fingers, massage in small pieces of butter until the mixture begins to look like coarse crumbs. Sprinkle crumbs evenly over muffins.

Bake for 20-25 minutes or until they test done with a toothpick.

Allow to cool for about 5 minutes inside the pans. Meanwhile, whisk together the glaze by combining sugar and lemon juice in a small bowl. Add a squeeze more lemon juice if you need to break down the sugar more.

Turn muffins out onto a wire rack and drizzle with glaze over the top while still warm.

Roaring Rhubarb Muffins

If you're not familiar with rhubarb, it is a delightful red stalk that comes into season during warmer months with a unique flavor that pairs well with strawberries. Uncooked, rhubarb is unimpressive but when manipulated a little, like in these muffins, the stalk releases sweet, juicy flavor notes and softens to a fruity texture. The walnuts add a bit of unexpected crunch.

Ingredients:

1-1/4 cups (180 g) flour

1 egg

1/2 cup and 2 tablespoons (113 g) brown sugar

1/2 teaspoon (3 g) baking soda

1/2 teaspoon (3 g) baking powder

1/4 teaspoon (2 g) salt

1/4 cup (60 ml) vegetable oil

1/2 teaspoon (3 ml) vanilla extract

1/2 cup (120 ml) buttermilk

3/4 cup (110 g) diced rhubarb

1/4 cup and 2 tablespoons (60 g) chopped walnuts

Topping:

1-1/2 teaspoons (8 ml) melted butter

2 tablespoons and 2 teaspoons (33 g) white sugar

1/2 teaspoon (3 g) ground cinnamon

Directions:

Heat your oven to 350 ° F (180 ° C). Prepare two 12 cup muffin tins by greasing or lining the cups with paper liners.

Combine the flour, baking soda, baking powder and salt in a medium bowl.

Using an electric mixer, beat the brown sugar, oil, egg, vanilla and buttermilk in a different bowl until fully combined and smooth.

Incorporate the dry ingredients into the wet until just moist.

Fold in the rhubarb and walnuts.

Scoop batter into the muffin cups and fill each almost all the way.

Mix together the melted butter, white sugar and cinnamon in a small bowl and sprinkle evenly amongst the top of the muffins.

Bake about 25 minutes or until muffins bounce back when lightly touched.

Allow muffins to rest in the pans for about 10 minutes before turning out onto a wire rack to cool completely.

Perfect Tea Muffins

These are a wonderful accompaniment to a cup of hot tea or coffee. The poppy seeds do a lot for the texture while the lemon and buttermilk give them a tart flavor.Serving them at the end of a nice dinner party gives you major party host points.

Ingredients:

1 1/3 cups (160 g) flour

2 large eggs , separated

1/2 cup (120 g) sweet creamy butter , softened

2/3 cup (130 g) sugar

1 teaspoon (5 g) baking powder

1/2 teaspoon (3 g) baking soda

2 tablespoons (40 g) poppy seeds

2 lemons, zest of , grated

1/4 teaspoon (2 g) salt

1/2 cup (120 ml) buttermilk or plain yogurt (120 g)

2 tablespoons (30 ml) lemon juice

1 teaspoon (5 ml) vanilla

Directions:

Heat oven to 350°F (180°C) and spray a 12 muffin cup tin lightly with cooking spray to prevent the muffins from sticking.

Beat together butter and sugar in a large bowl until it reaches a fluffy consistency.

Incorporate egg yolks one at a time, beating well after each addition.

Combine flour, baking powder, baking soda, poppy seeds, and lemon zest in a separate bowl.

Incorporate the dry ingredients into the wet mixture on low speed in your mixer. Alternate this step twice adding the buttermilk, then lemon juice, and then vanilla. Beat until just smooth. Do not over-mix.

Using a hand mixer, beat egg whites in a separate bowl until stiff peaks form and fold them carefully into the muffin batter just until blended to maintain airiness.

Carefully scoop batter into the tin, filling each muffin cup about ¾ of the way up.

Bake for 20-25 minutes or until a toothpick comes out clean when inserted into the middle.

Allow to cool for 5 minutes in the pan before turning out onto a wire rack to cool completely.

Sweet as a Peach Muffins

During the peak of summer, when peaches are at their juiciest and sweetest, these muffins are a great way to showcase this delicious fruit. While the recipe works with canned peaches, it just has so much more appeal with fresh. This recipe is something to look forward to during the hotter months. Just crack a window or turn on the AC and turn that oven up.

Ingredients:

3 cups (360 g) all-purpose flour

3 eggs, lightly beaten

2 cups (400 g) white sugar

1 tablespoon (15 g) ground cinnamon

1 teaspoon (5 g) baking soda

1 teaspoon (8 g) salt

1 1/4 cups (290 ml) vegetable oil

2 cups peeled (300 g), pitted, and chopped peaches

Directions:

Preheat oven to 400 ° F (200 ° C). Lightly grease 12 large muffin cups or line them with paper liners.

Sift flour, cinnamon, baking soda, and salt into a large mixing bowl.

Using a different bowl, combine your wet ingredients by stirring together the oil, eggs, and sugar.

Add the wet ingredients into the dry just until incorporated.

Gently fold in the peaches until coated in batter

Distribute batter amongst 12 prepared muffins cups evenly.

Bake for 25 minutes or until a tester inserted into the center comes out clean.

Allow to cool in the pan for about10 minutes.

Turn out onto a wire rack to continue cooling.

Blank Slate Corn Muffins

These basic corn muffins carry savory or sweet flavors well. Cornmeal creates a back drop for just about any add-in you can think of. From jalapenos to more subtle bell peppers, blueberries to cheddar cheese, these little goods of baked perfection can be eaten for breakfast, used instead of biscuits with dinner and dipped into a tomato bisque at lunch.

Ingredients:

1 cup (120 g) all-purpose flour

1 egg, beaten

1/3 cup (65 g) white sugar

1 cup (160 g) cornmeal

2 teaspoons (10 g) baking powder

1/2 teaspoon (4 g) salt

1/4 cup (60 ml) canola oil

1 cup (250 ml) milk

Directions:

Heat oven to 400 ° F (200 ° C).

Lightly grease a 12 muffin pan with butter, spray with cooking spray or line the cups with paper muffin liners.

Stir together corn meal, flour, sugar, baking powder and salt in a large bowl.

In a smaller bowl, gently stir together egg, oil and milk until combined.

Fold in whatever add-ins you decide to use. Diced jalapenos give these a savory kick. Go the sweet route with fresh blueberries.

Pour batter into muffin cups. If you folded in a savory ingredient, go all out and sprinkle a bit of cheddar and a bit of coarse salt on top of each muffin before placing them in the oven.

Bake for 15 to 20 minutes or until a tester inserted into the middle comes out clean.

11 Tips for Awesome Muffins

Muffins are a great entry into the baking world as the basic method is simple: mix wet ingredients, mix dry ingredients then combine dry into wet, stir and bake. Of course there is much variation on the basic method and with the following tips, you can master the art of muffin making pretty quickly and start adding your own creative twists.

* Never mix the batter too much. Once the dry ingredients are in the wet, all you want to do is mix them together enough until everything is moistened. What happens if you over-mix? The air pockets in the batter fall flat and you end up with a round brick.

* Since muffins hang out in the middle of the bread-to-cake continuum, tweaking certain ingredients will bring you close to one end of the spectrum than the other. The less butter and sugar you add, the more bread-like the consistency of the muffins and vice versa.

* Make sure the ingredients you start with are at room temperature. This is important because they will blend better without extra mixing required.

* Divide up your mixing tools: use a fork to mix the dry ingredients, a whisk to mix the wet and a rubber spatula to fold in any add-ins (like fruit and nuts).

* When folding in add-ins, incorporate them gently until just coated in batter then give it one final stir and put down the spatula. Seriously.

* Big flour pockets are bad. Small lumps are completely fine.

* If your batter is lumpy (due to add-in), it's best to use an ice cream scoop or a large spoon to place the batter into muffin tins.

* Make muffin tops (the undisputed best part of the muffin) by overfilling the muffin cups a little bit. When they bake up, the batter will rise and form a fluffy muffin top. Make sure to coat the tin (including the spaces in between cups) with cooking spray before filling it with batter so that you can easily remove your muffins when they're done.

* Aim for even heat distribution in your oven by either a) positioning your oven rack in the middle or if you're making several batches at once, b) switching the top and bottom pan positions half way through baking.

* This one is hard but you must let your muffins cool and settle for a few minutes before removing them from the pans.

* Muffins freeze well. Just wrap them individually in plastic wrap and throw them in the freezer for up to 2 months. When you are ready to use them again, place them on the counter to thaw, still wrapped. Then warm them in a warm oven for a few minutes to bring them back to life.

THE END

It's the end of the muffins story. Thank you so much for investing in this book. These essential muffin recipes are all you need to bake any muffin recipes. Just change few ingredients and get the flavor you want in to create your own new delicious muffins.

I hope you now have the inspiration to bake those muffins for your close ones, and for yourself too! So turn up the oven and...

Happy Muffin Baking,

Mary :)

5792543R00033

Printed in Great Britain
by Amazon.co.uk, Ltd.,
Marston Gate.